Project Homepage

Pencil Drawings
July 2013-August 2014

Iris M. Kirkwood
artist, writer

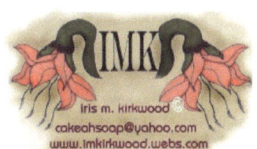

First Edition

1.

The Artist-

Iris M. Kirkwood is an African American woman native to Buffalo New York. Self taught Iris considers herself a consummate student of life. Combining observation with an innate story telling ability, she calls her style Visual Narratives. Her work has been shown in galleries all along the East coast.

The Pencil Drawings-

The pencil drawings presented in this book take bits and pieces of memories and dreams to create Visual Narratives. In July of 2013 the series started with common items drawn in a collage of images that were fantasy, dreamlike in their presentation. But as the year progressed into 2014 random bits of memory began to dominate the drawings theme. Always there are fantastical elements used along with the tools for telling short stories - that is character, setting and point of view.

This is an on going series that continues to evolve as it grows.

The Pencil Drawings

Dreams mixed with memories

Make fantastic associations.

The mix sometimes

Creates a frightening combination.

Trying to force a clear memory

Some-times make a lie.

iris m. kirkwood

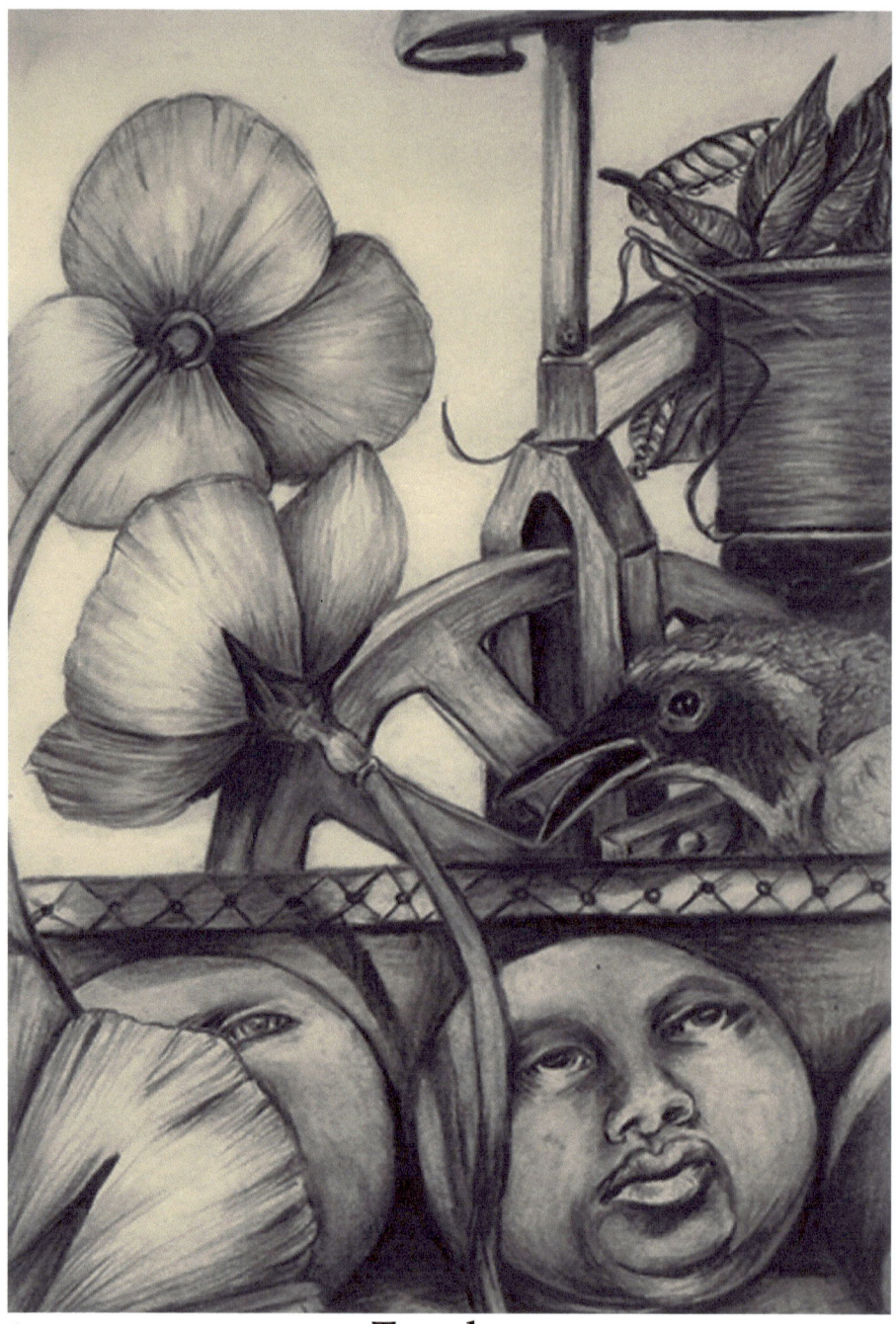

Tuesday

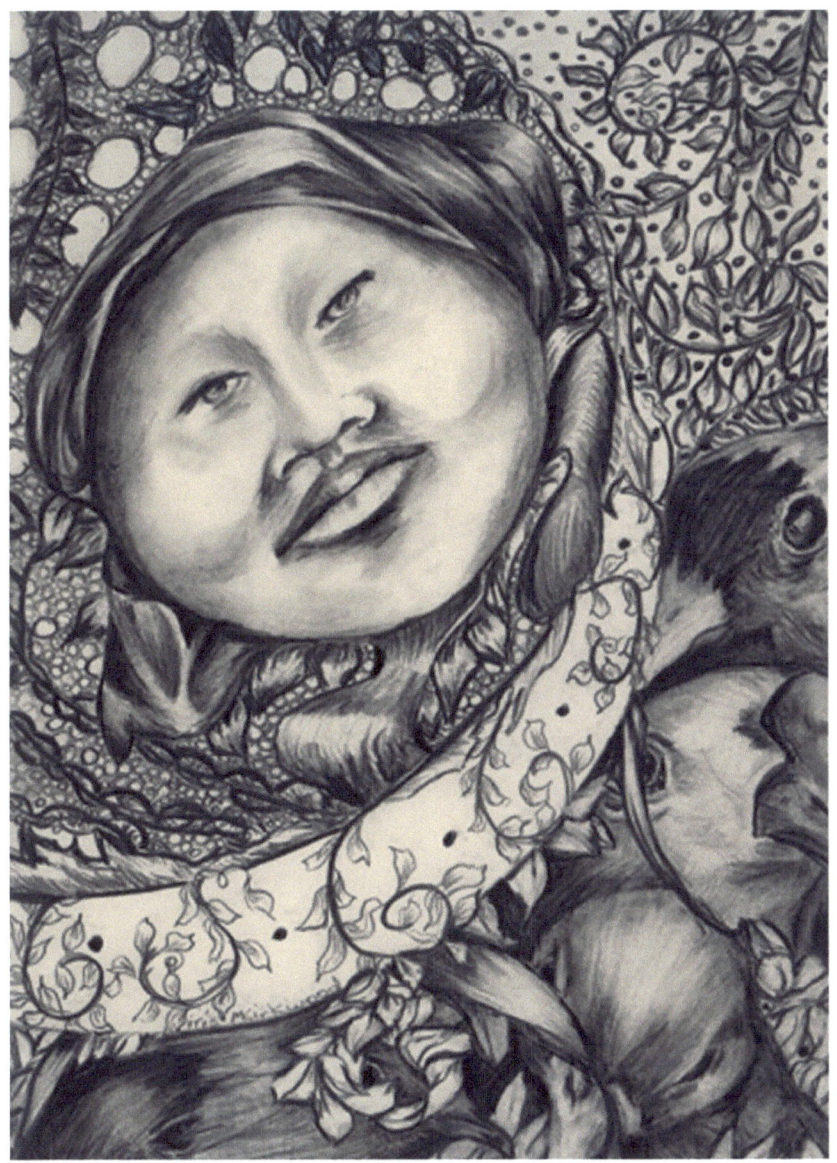

Morning

Noon

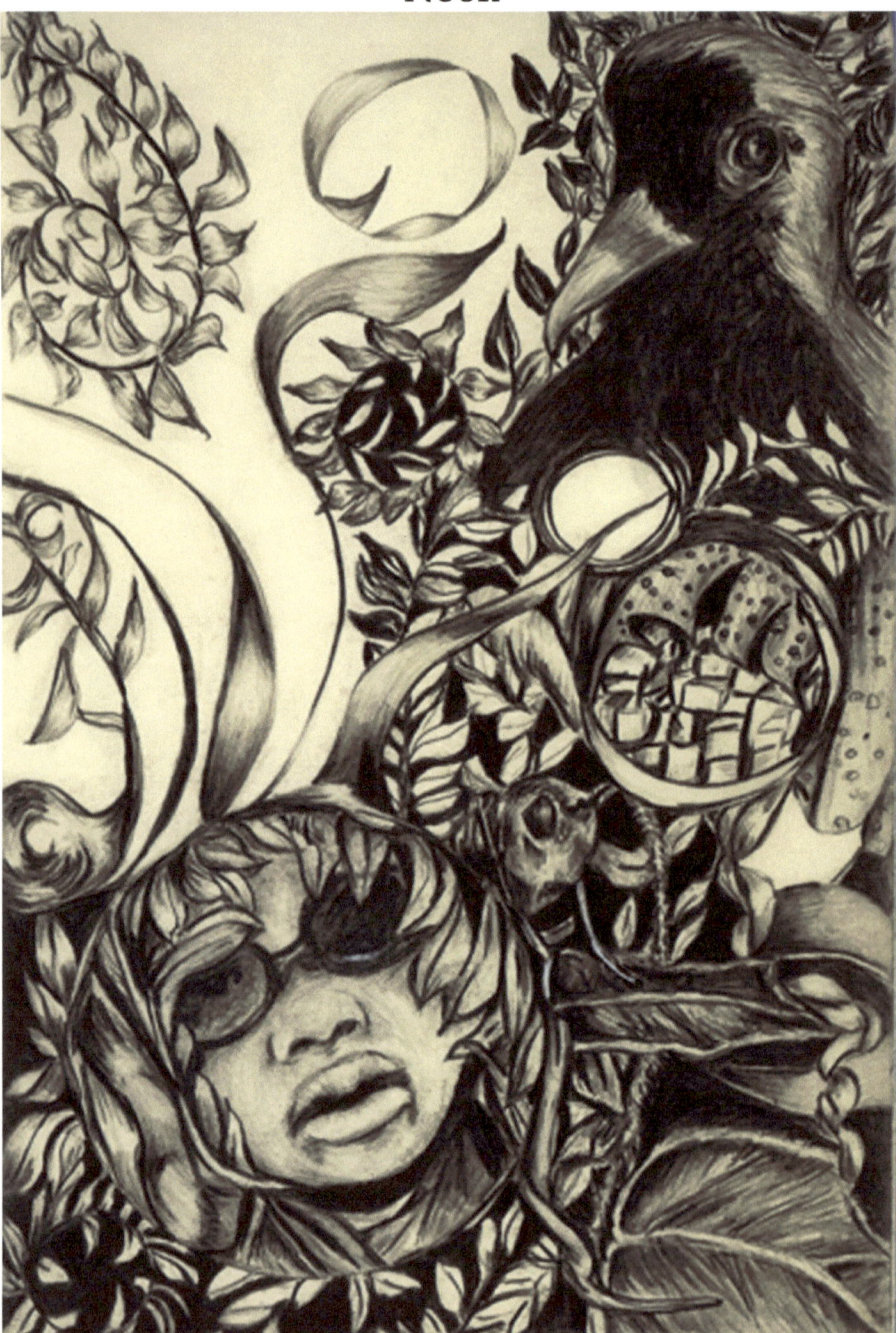

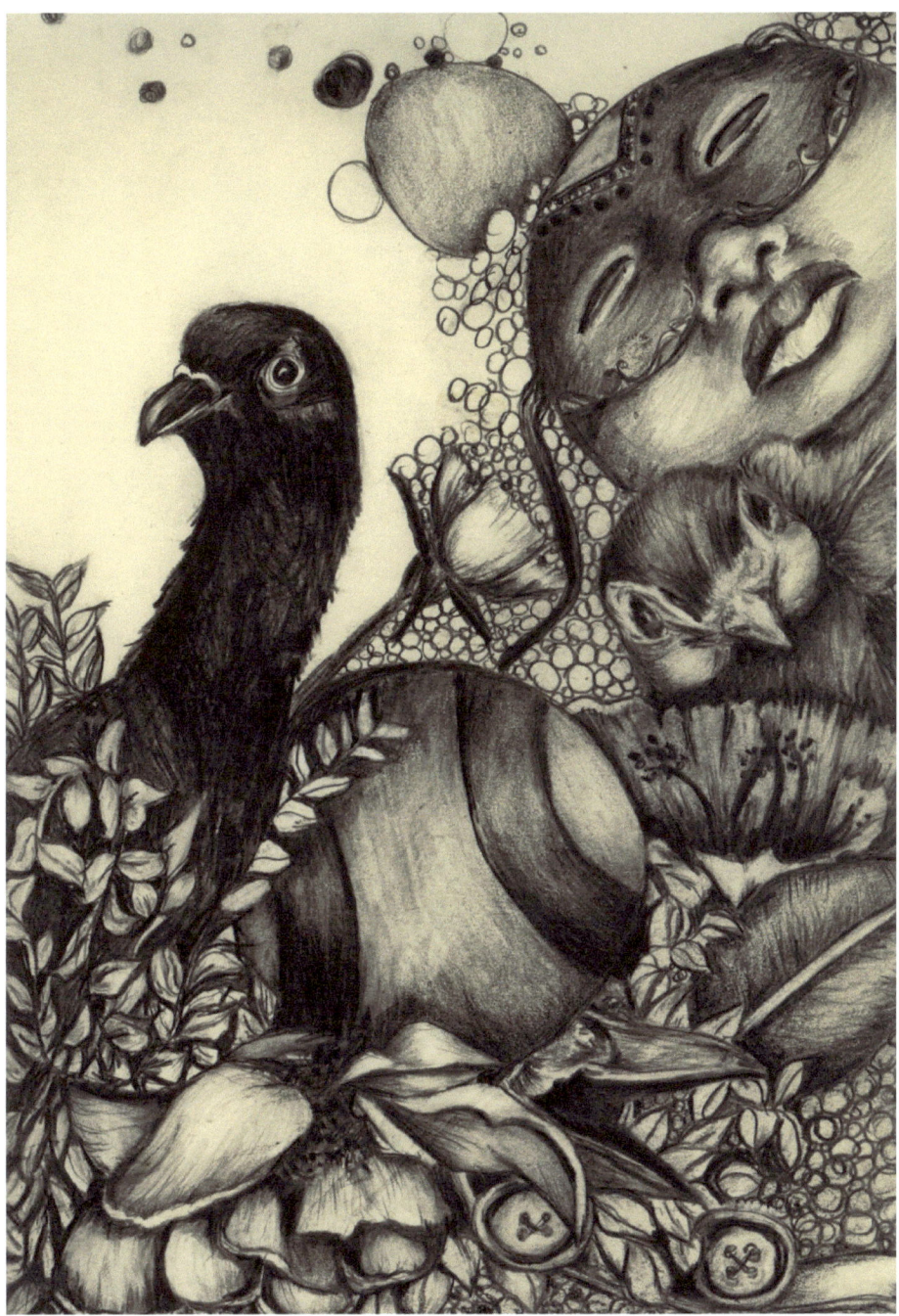

Night

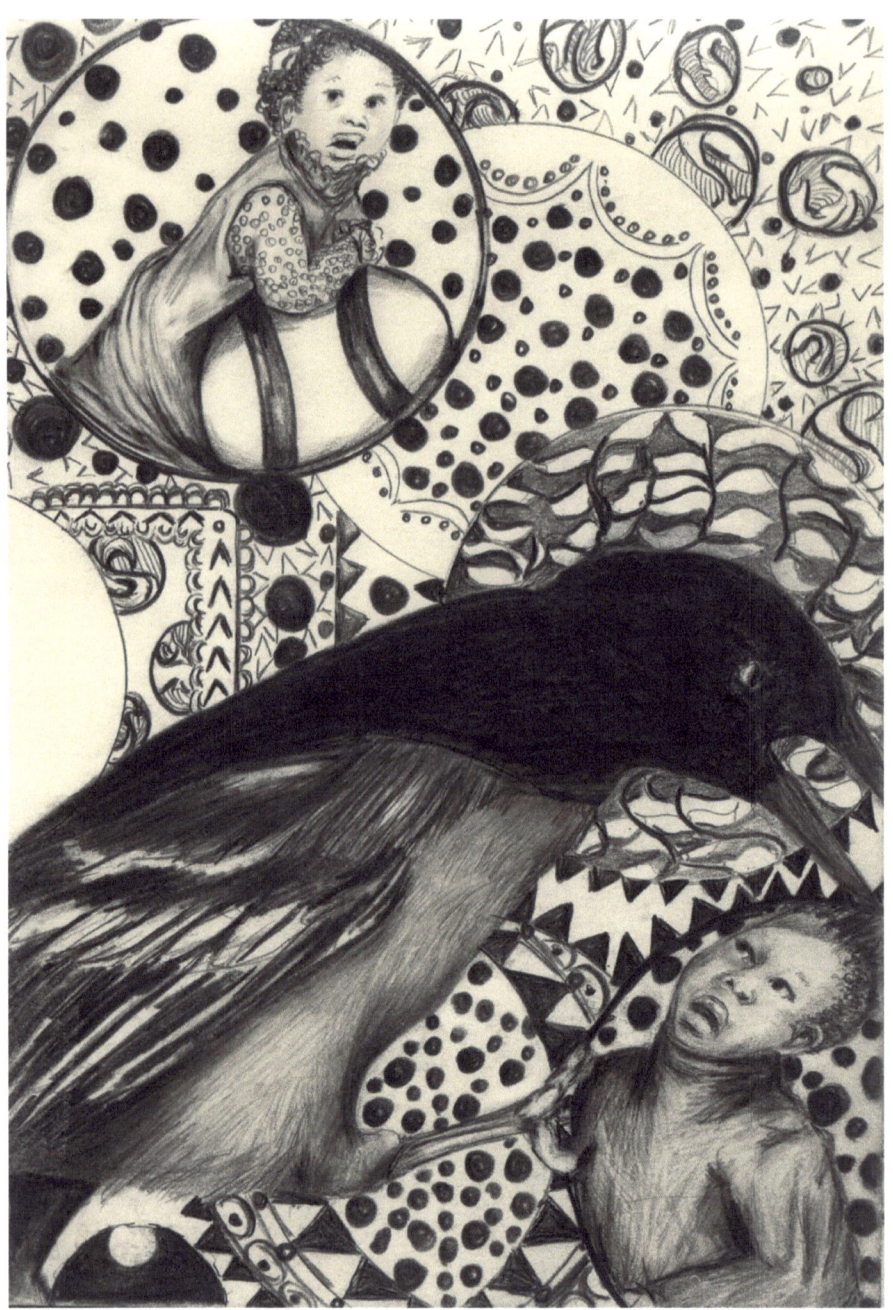

The Messenger

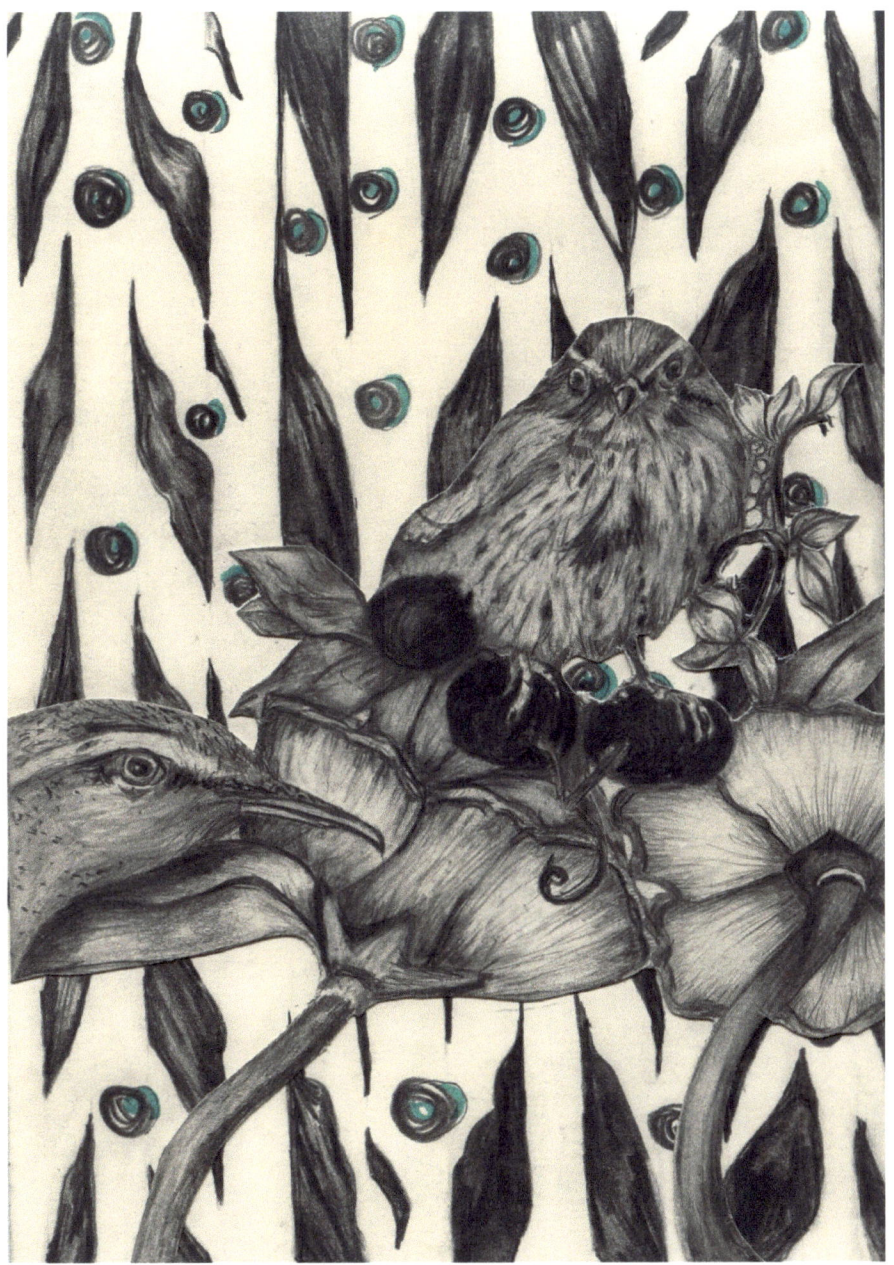

Mine

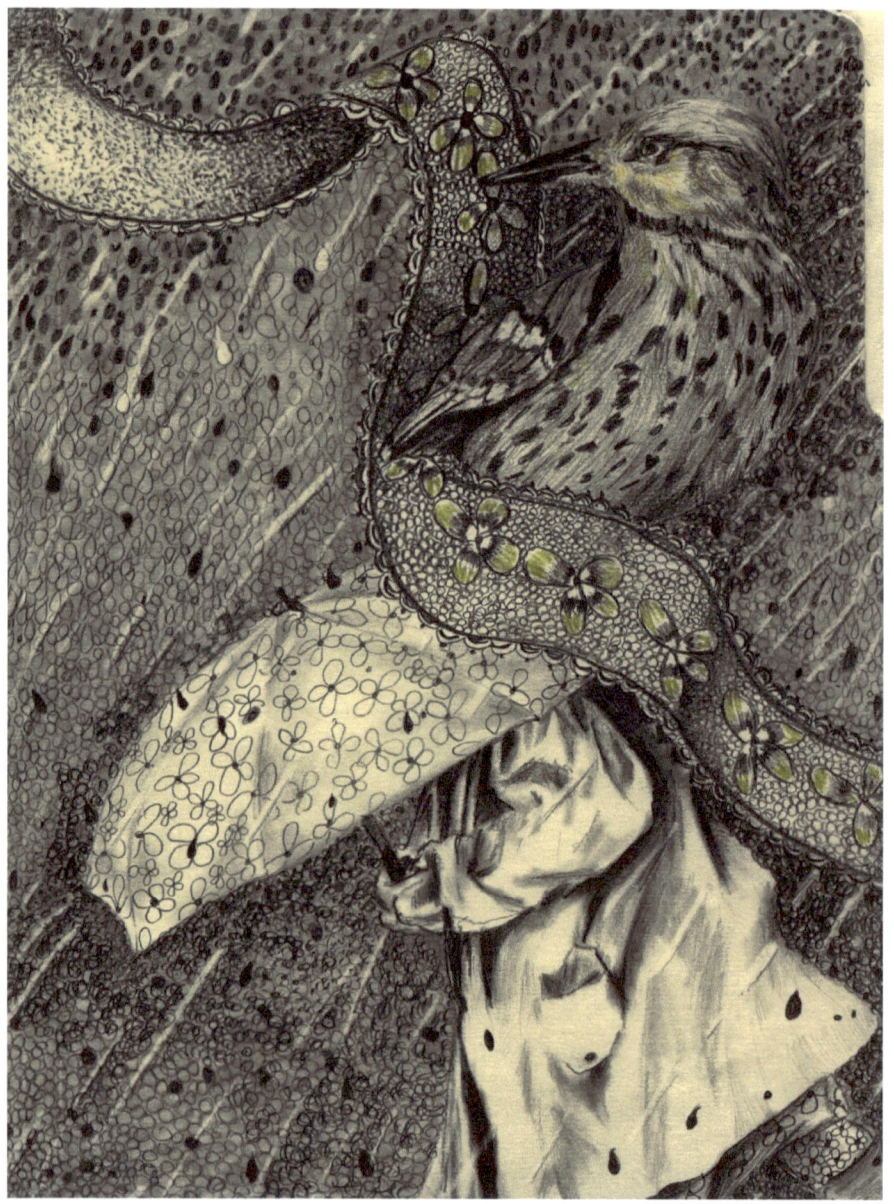

Heavy Rain

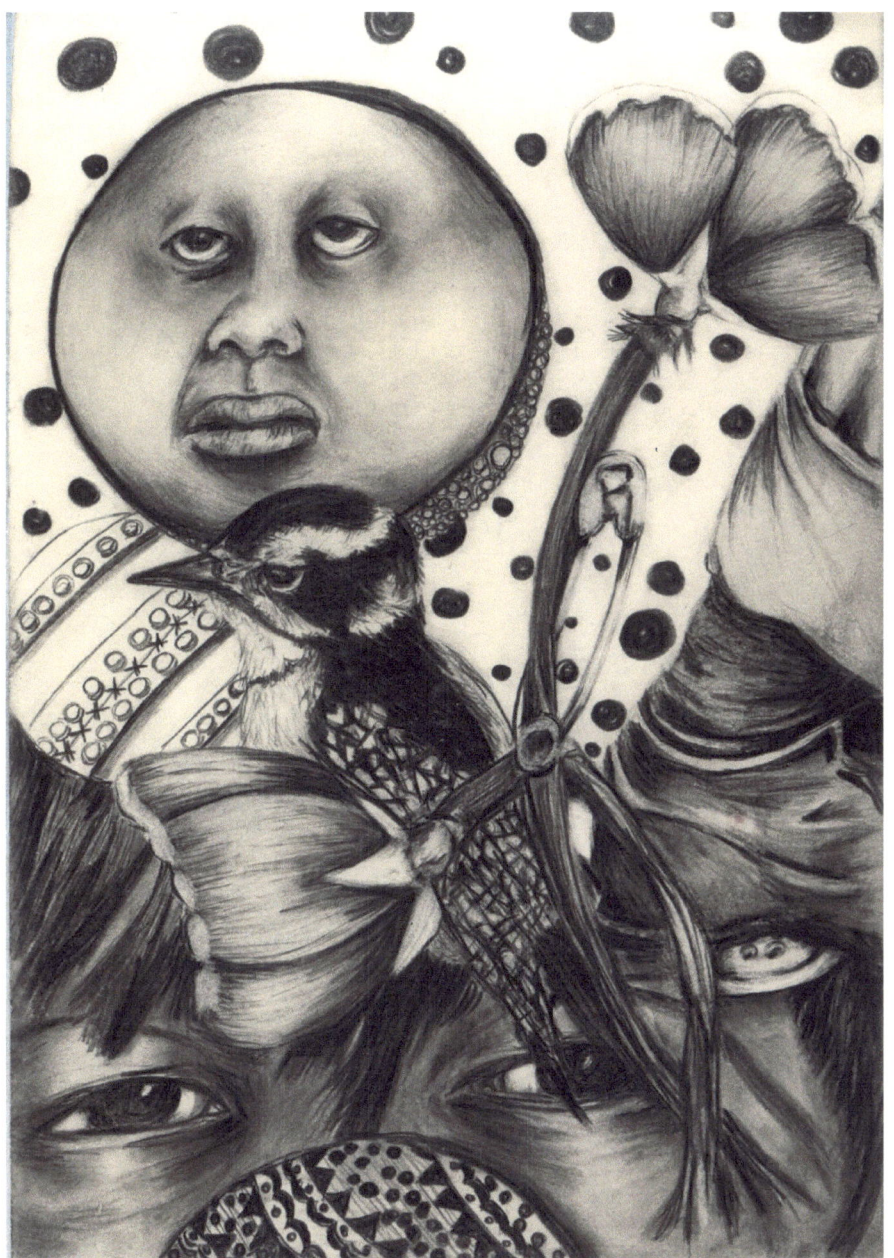

Hold It Together

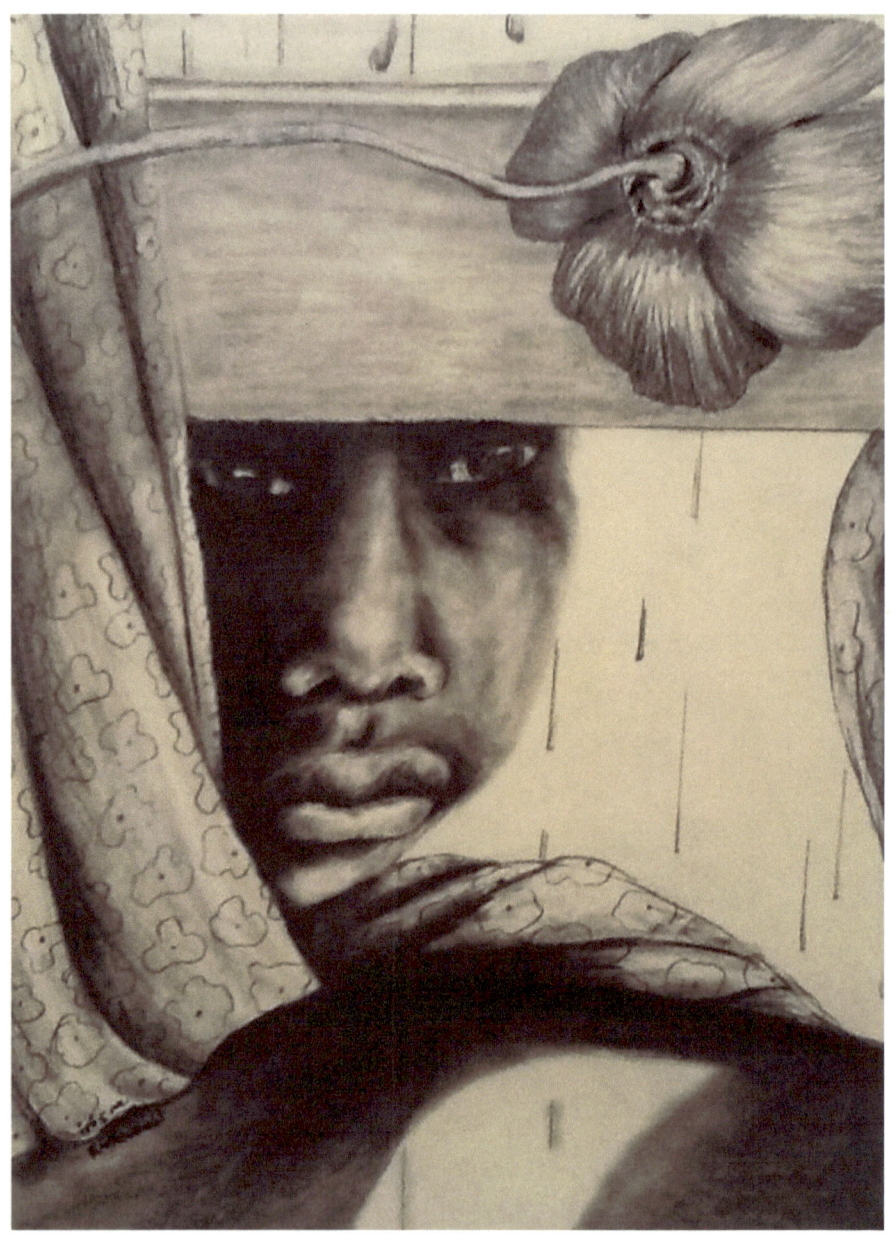

Not on The Outside

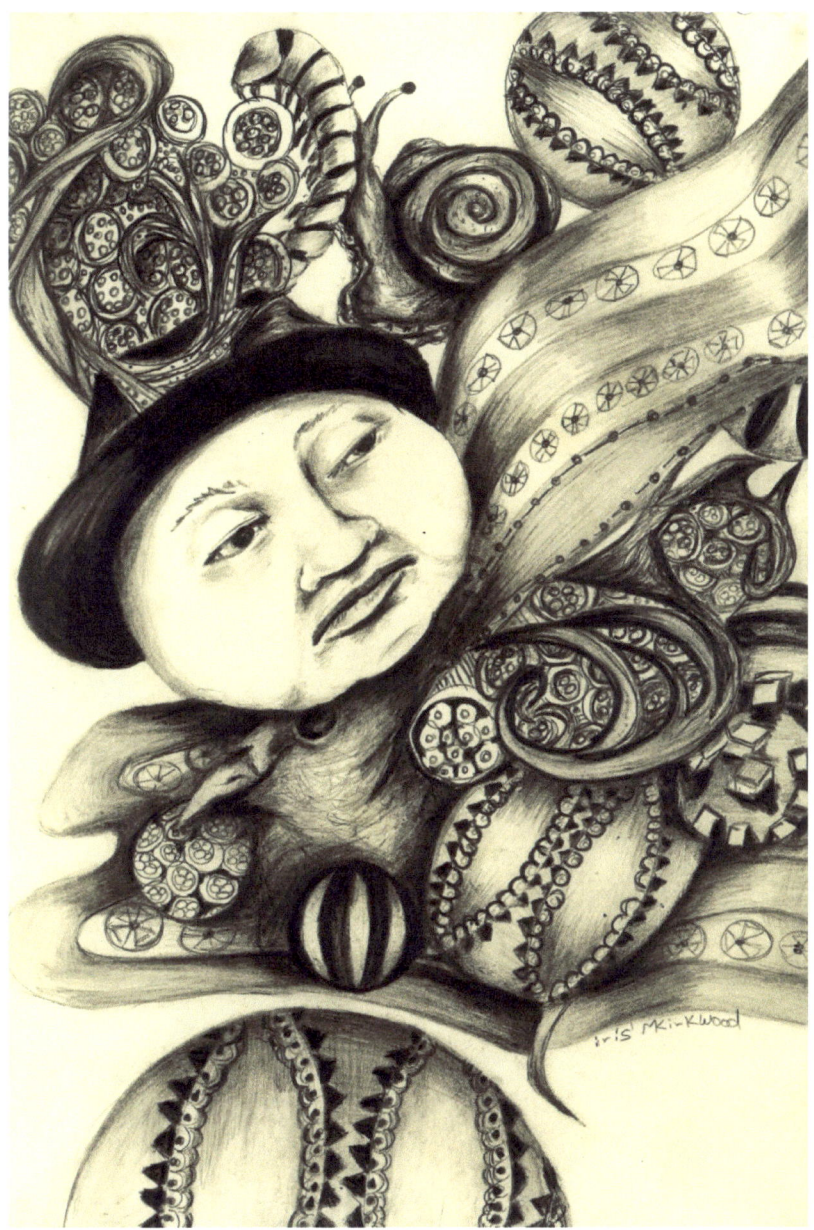

Silk

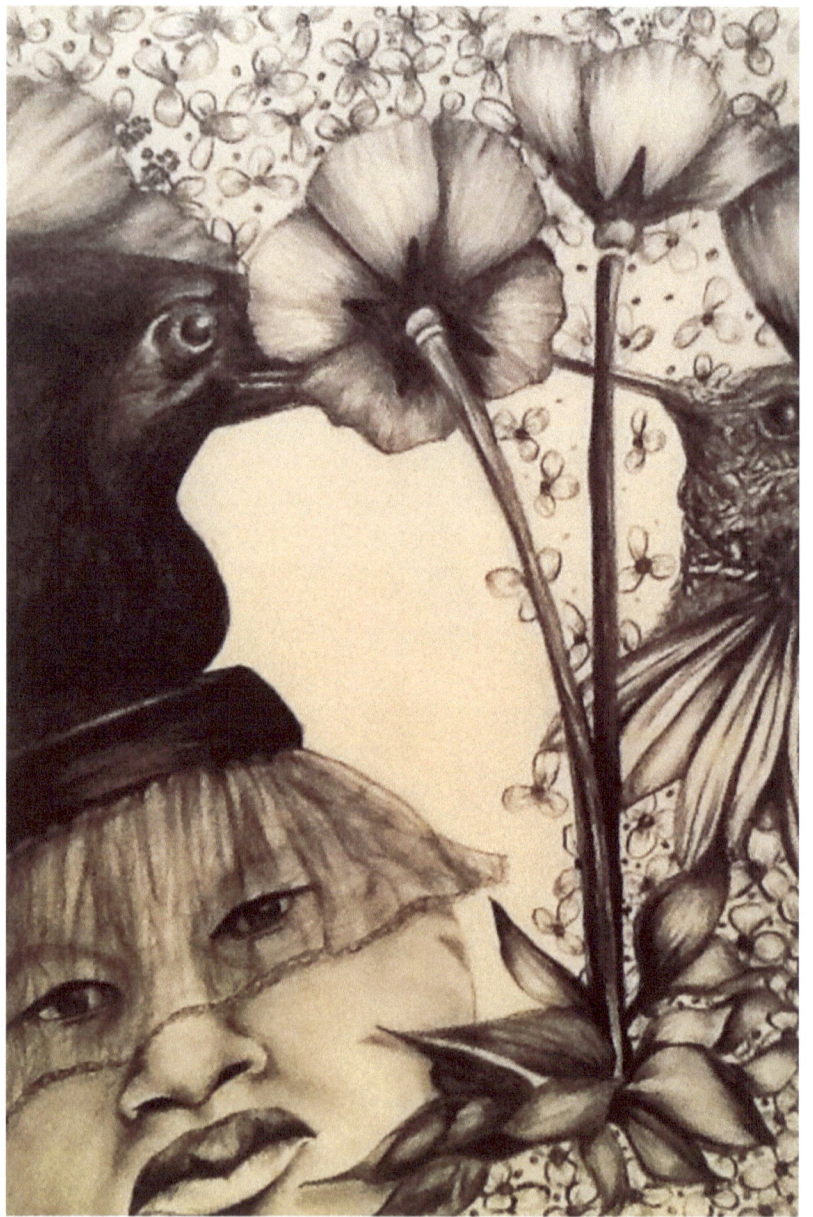

Poppies

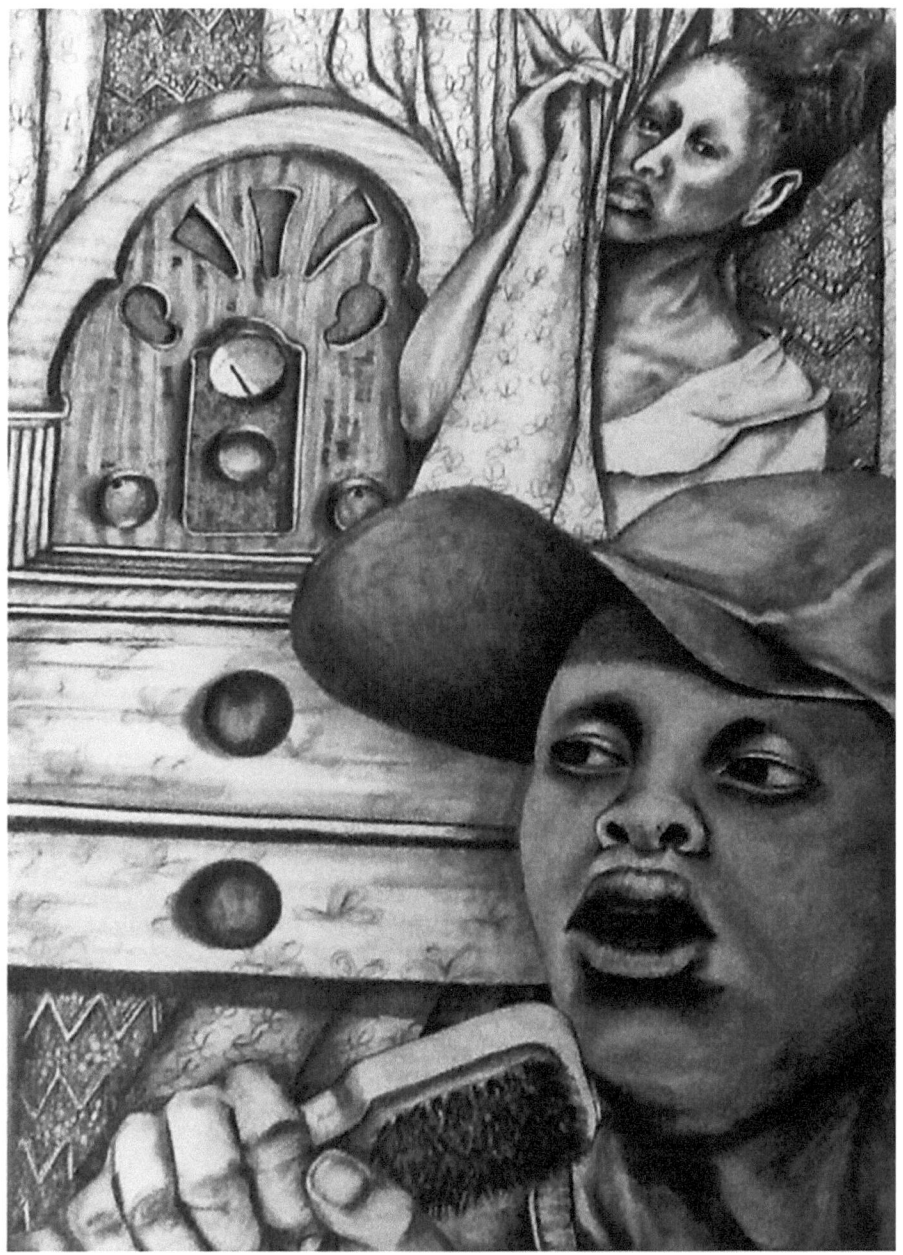

The Dreamer Sings

Three Ladles and a face

In the August 1991 issue
of Victoria magazine
I saw the photograph of a
jacket buttoned
in this fashion.
The photograph has
become my muse.
I've used this jacket
in several drawings
from this series.

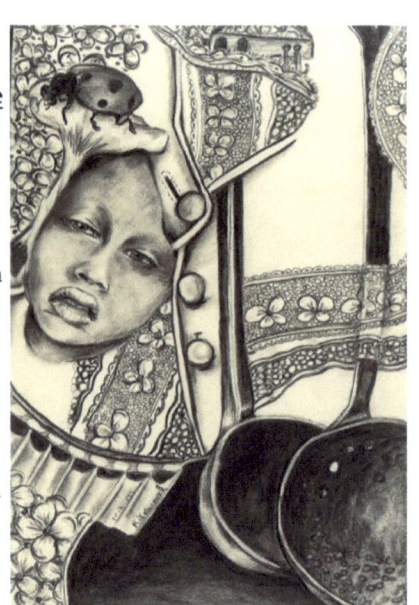

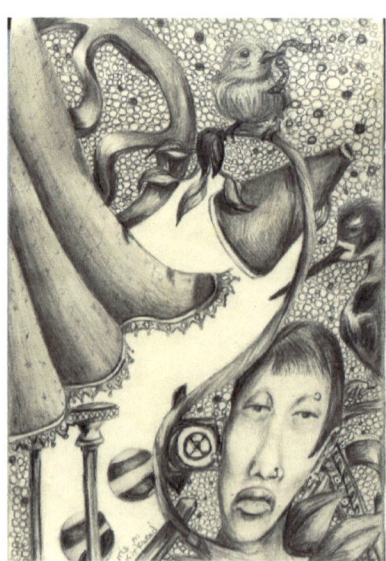

And Then

Sometimes I find the
shape of the jacket
has made its way
into my drawing
without
my planning it.

16

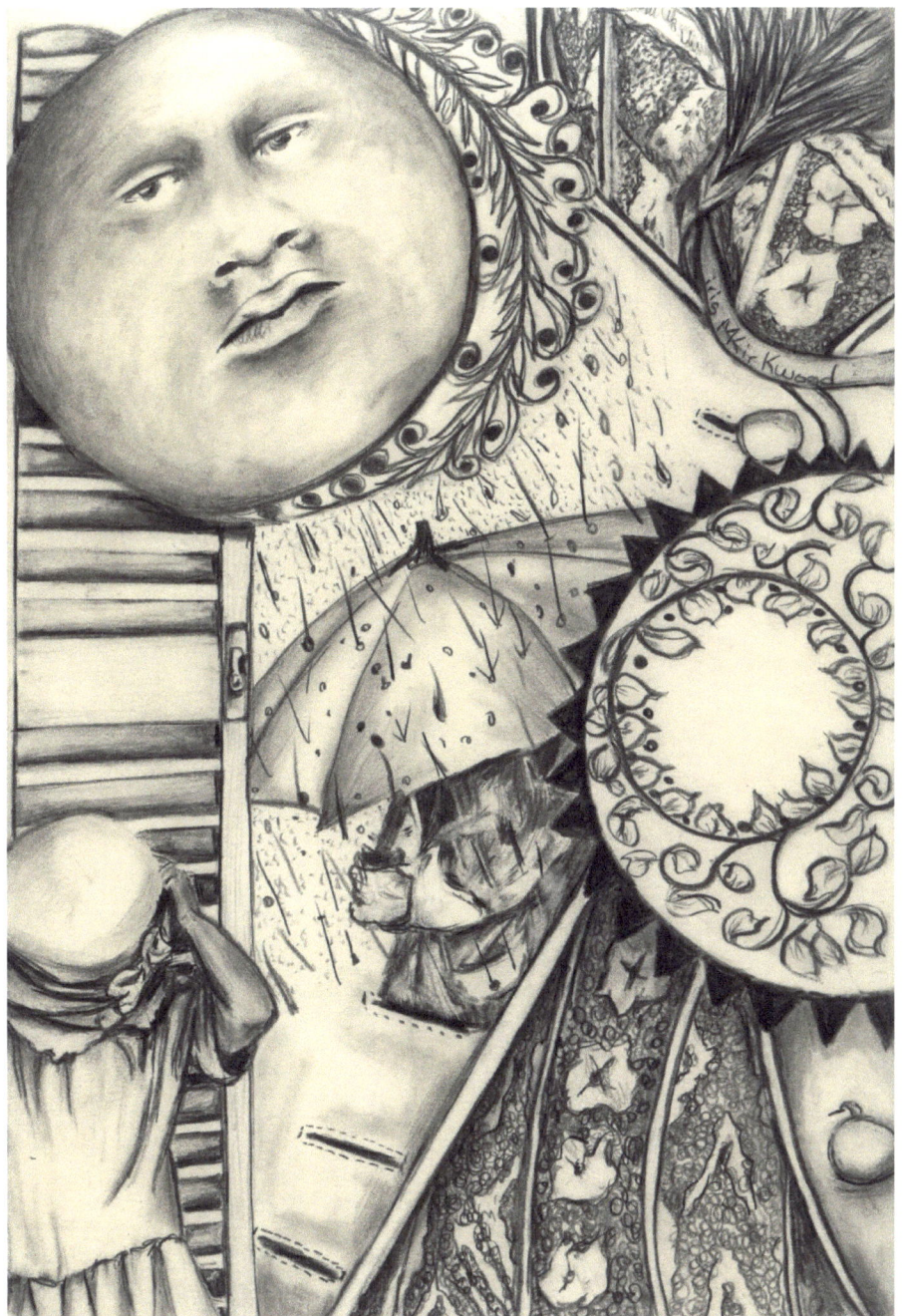

Pitter Patter

I See It

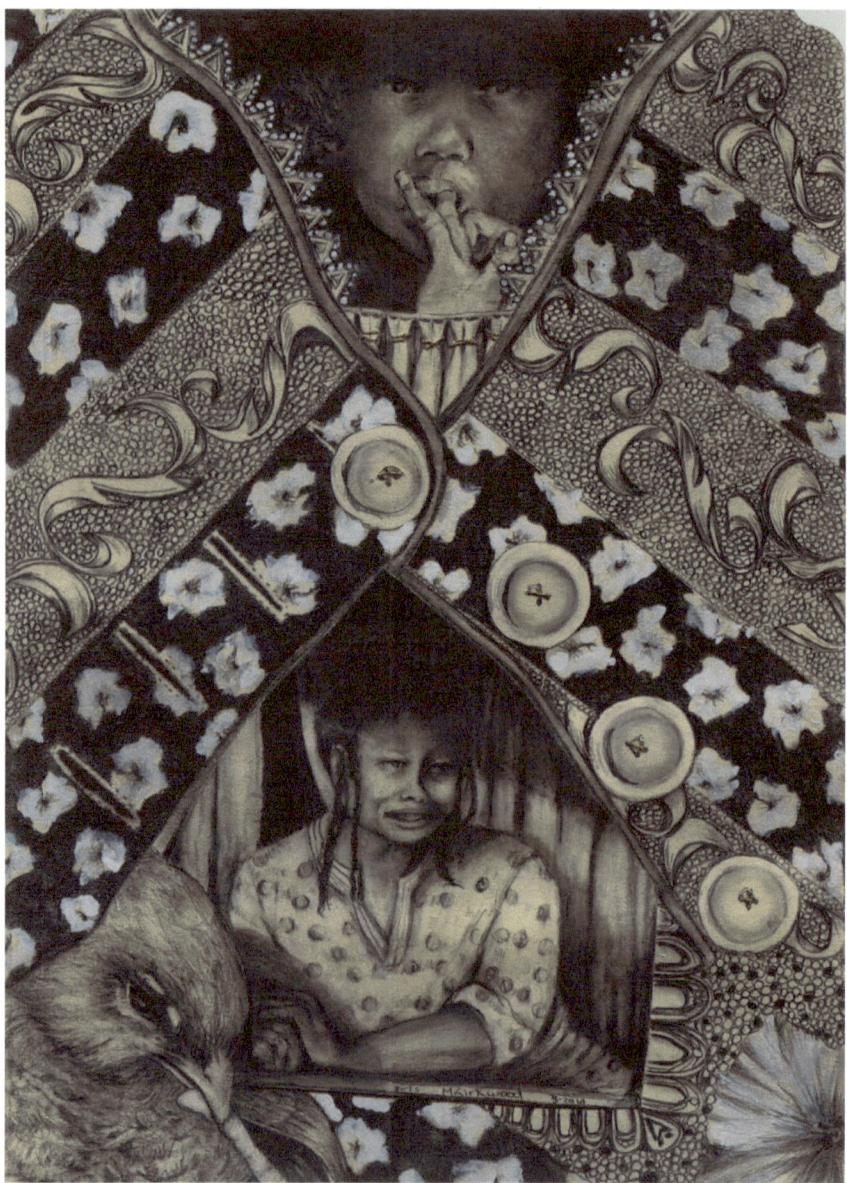

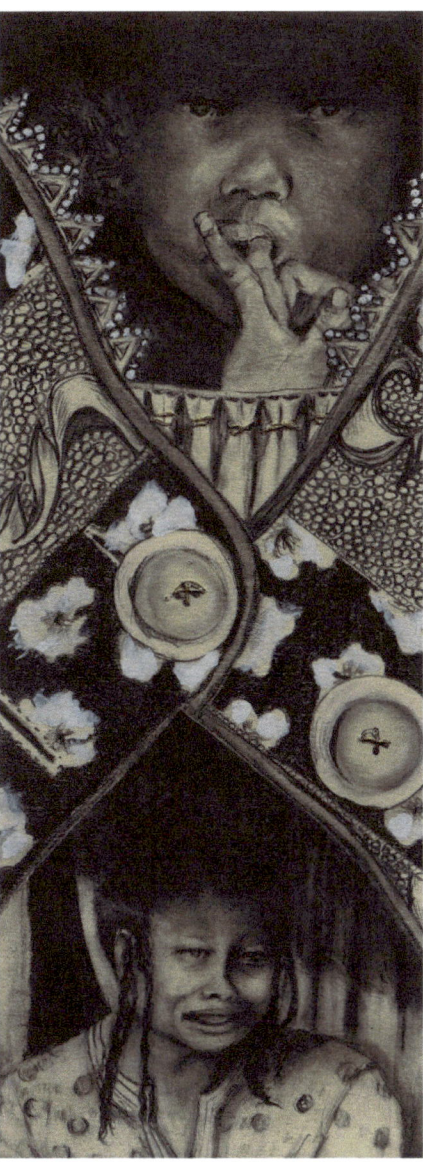

Detail:
I See It

This jacket shape has inspired me to create some very interesting visual narratives.

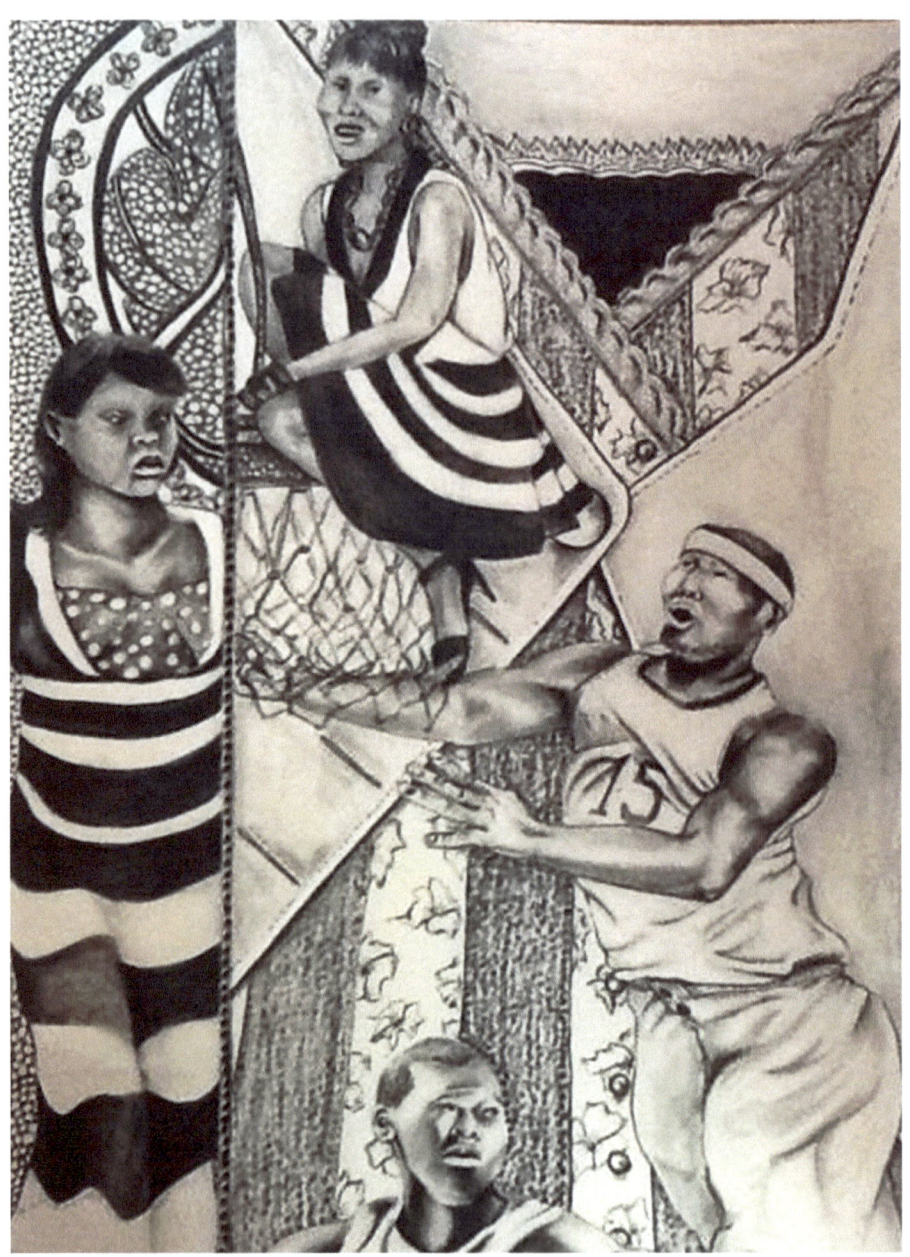

The Object to Score

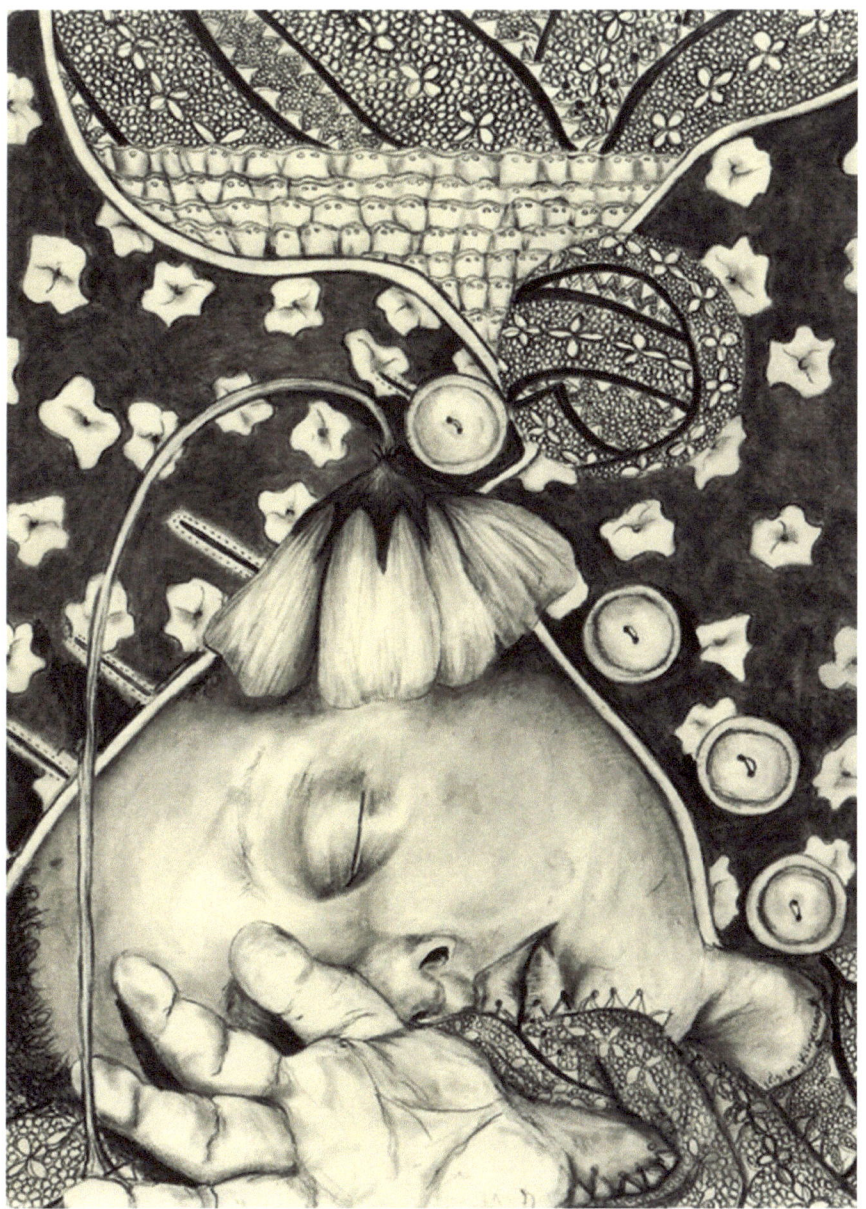

Conjure

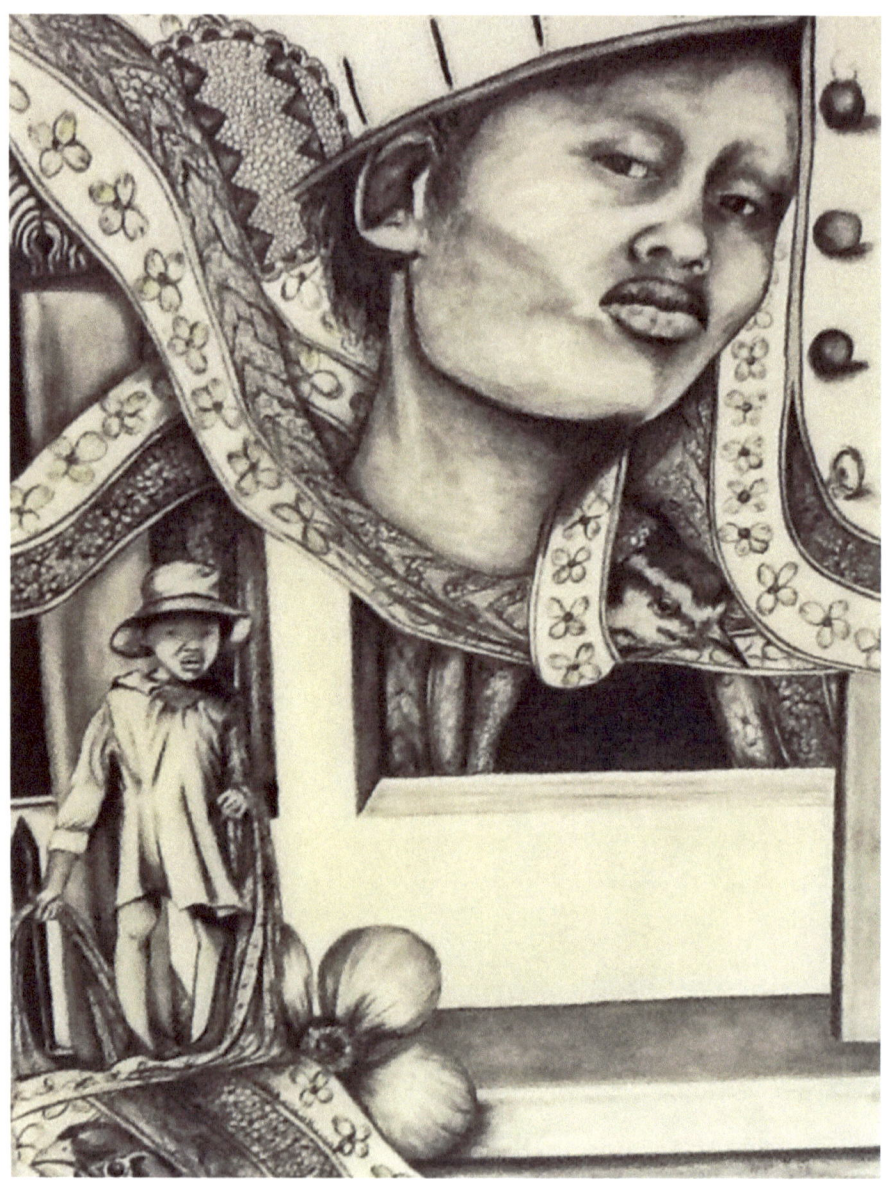

Forget Me Not

My Mother Myself

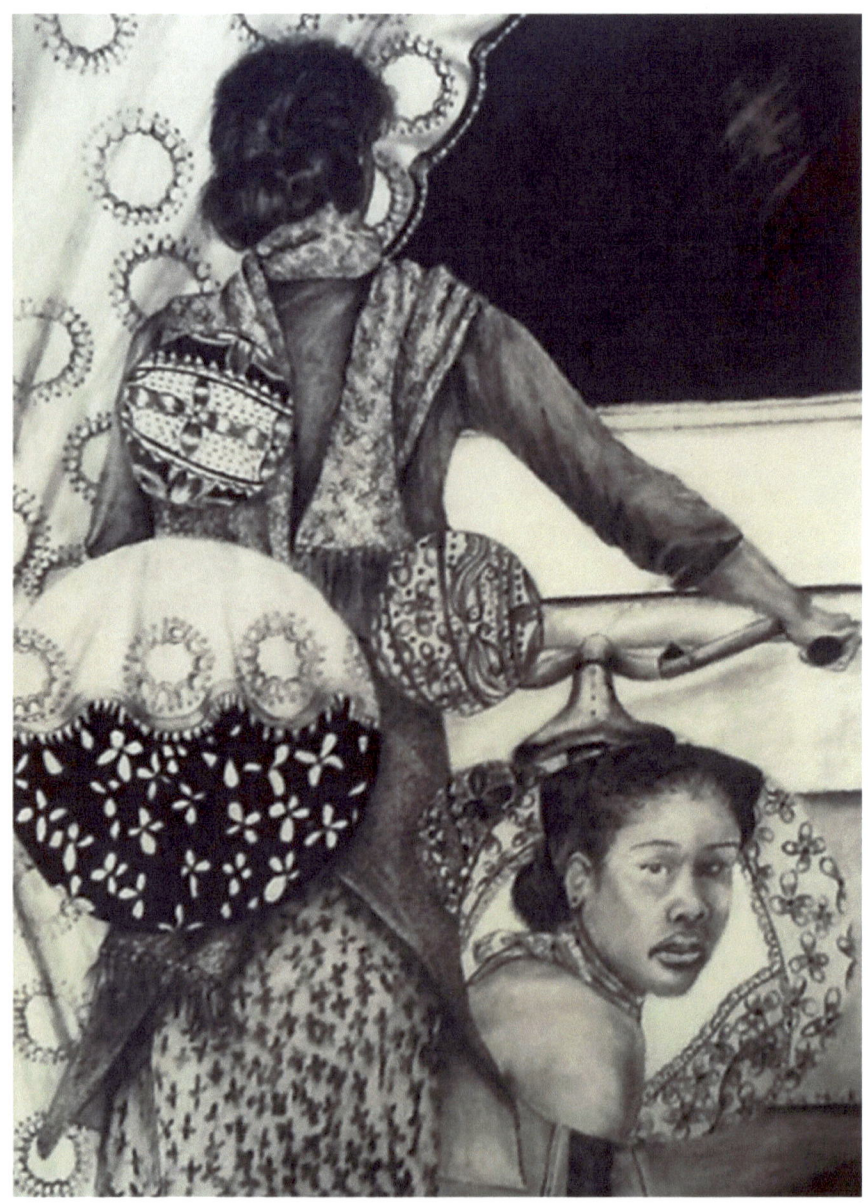

Now What

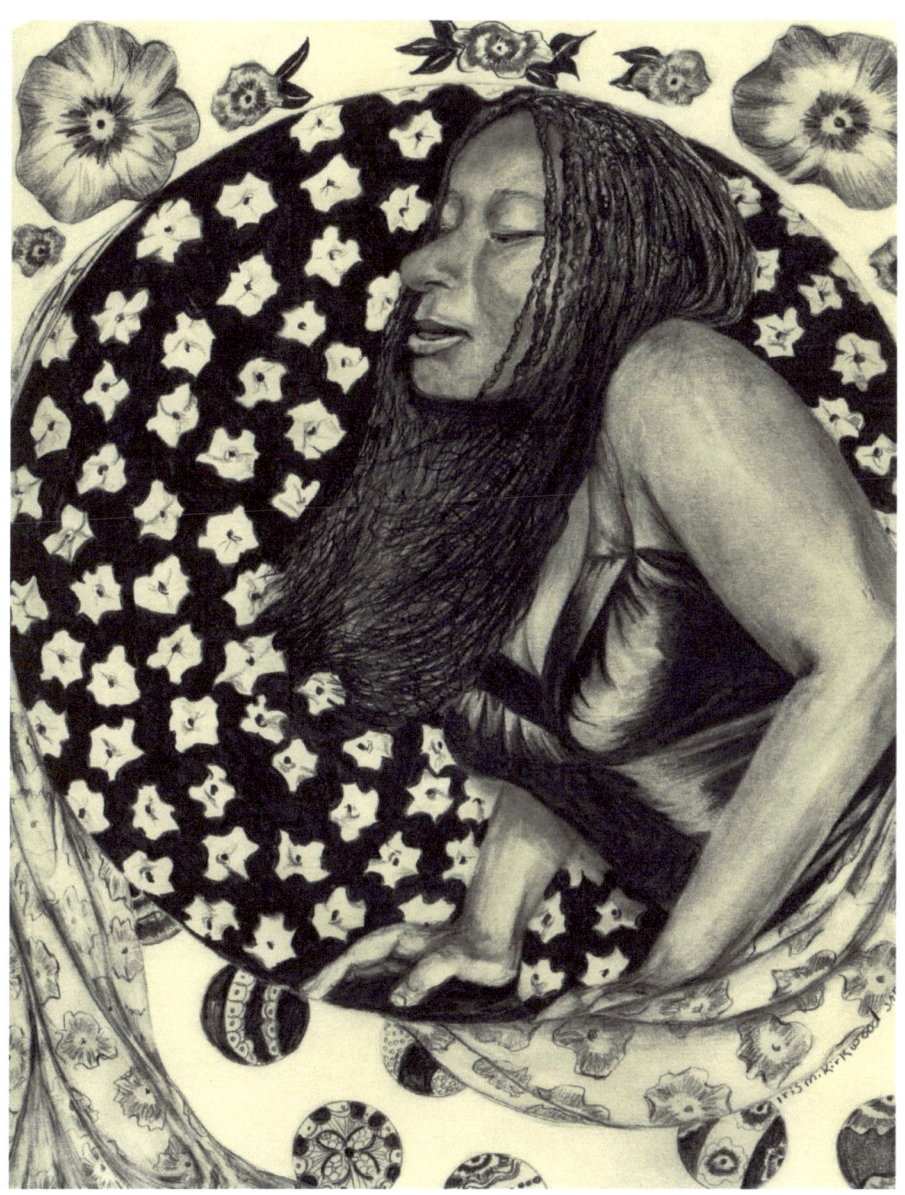

Perched

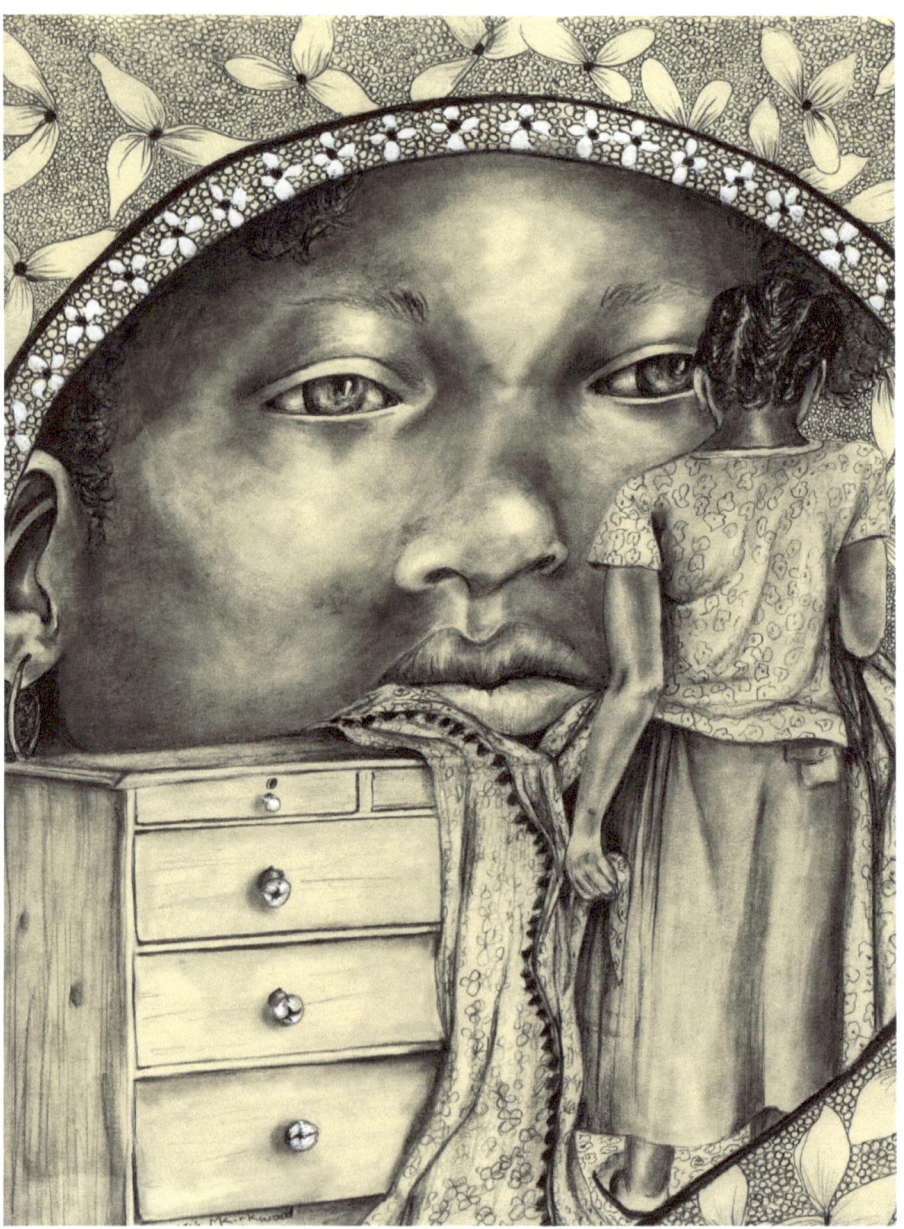

Past Tears

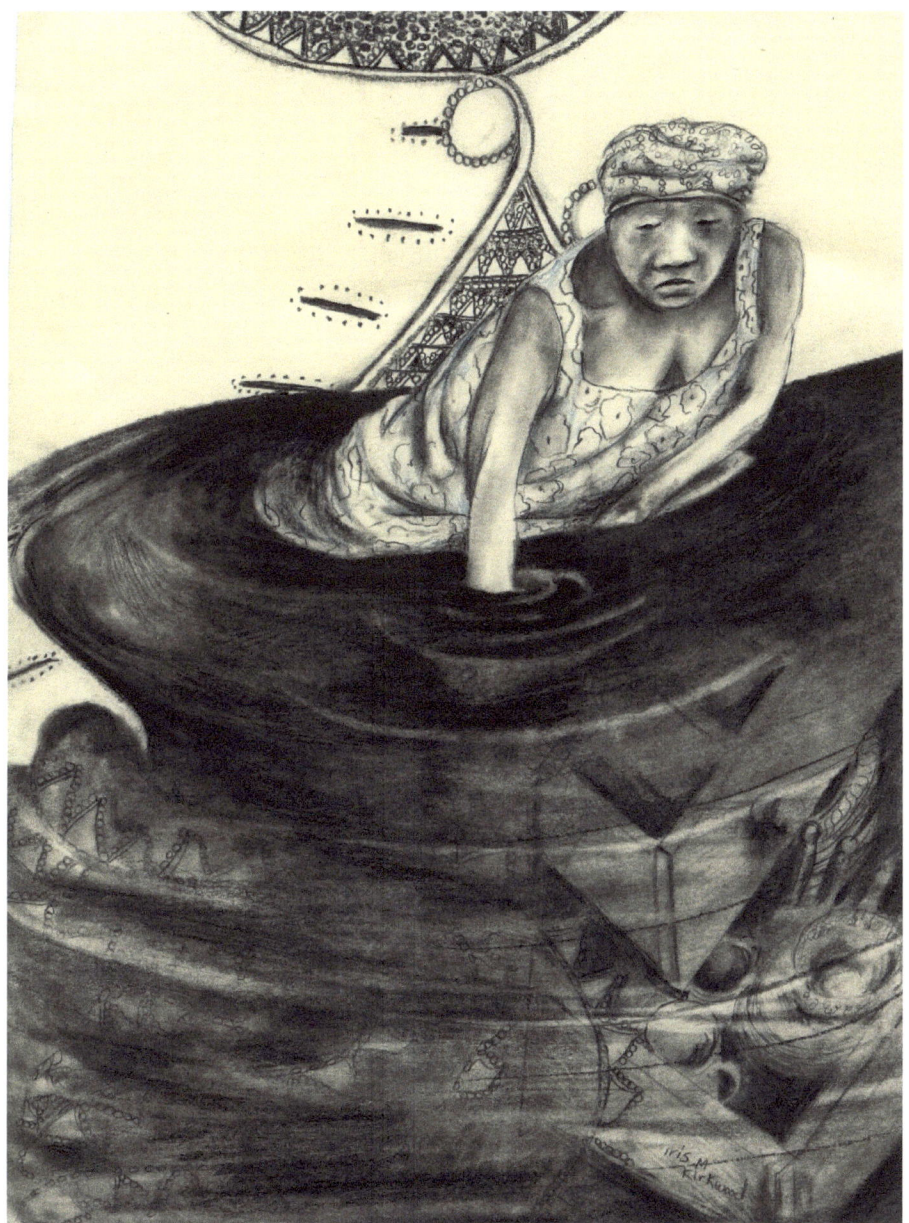

I'm here Somewhere

A Last Word

The use of Birds, flowers and fabric throughout this series are a reflection of the artist's own vague memories and dreams. Iris accepts that these particular elements are an important aspect of her creative spirit. But why, and how it came to be-she cannot explain.

Often Iris uses Manila file folders to draw on. She finds it interesting to use something that was specifically created for 'filing away information' to draw her dreams and bits of memory on.

To see more work from this artist:
www.imkirkwood.webs.com

www.ingramcontent.com/pod-product-compliance
Lightning Source LLC
Chambersburg PA
CBHW040915180526
45159CB00010BA/3075